Let's Take a Trip
An Outward Bound School

by Alison Murray Kuller

photography by Tom Stewart

Troll Associates

Library of Congress Cataloging-in-Publication Data

Kuller, Alison Murray.
    An outward bound school / by Alison Murray Kuller; photography by
Thomas R. Stewart and Alison Murray Kuller.
       p.   cm.—(Let's take a trip)
    Summary: Text and photographs highlight the activities at the
Hurricane Island Outward Bound School off the coast of Maine as
students face the challenges of nature, discover personal strengths,
and learn the value of team work.
    ISBN 0-8167-1731-1 (lib. bdg.)   ISBN 0-8167-1732-X (pbk.)
    1. Hurricane Island Outward Bound School—Juvenile literature.
[1. Hurricane Island Outward Bound School. 2. Outward bound
schools.] I. Stewart, Thomas R., ill. II. Title. III. Series.
GV200.54.M2K85 1990
796.54'22—dc20   89-5169

The author and publisher wish to thank Carole Ryder, Tino O'Brien, and the rest of the staff of the
Hurricane Island Outward Bound School for their generous assistance and cooperation, and to
acknowledge the Hurricane Island Outward Bound School for the photographs on pages 9, 24, and 28.

Years ago, when sailors headed for unknown territories, they gave the call "Outward Bound!" Today, young people share that excitement as they arrive at the Hurricane Island Outward Bound School in Rockland, Maine. Each group or *watch* of ten students meets with the two instructors who will be leading the 18-day course. Let's join a watch and find out what will happen when they get to Hurricane Island.

First, students gather everything they will need for the trip to Hurricane Island. They pack their clothes, sea boots, foul-weather gear, and life jackets. Together they stock the 30-foot-long *pulling boat* with food, charts, compass, and sleeping bags. With no cabin to protect them in rain or wind, students carefully stash rain gear close by!

Before the watch sets sail, the instructors need to
make sure that everyone can swim, so the entire
watch takes part in a swim test. Each student
jumps off the float and swims 25 yards.
Nonswimmers use life jackets.

Outward Bound is *experiential education*, which means that students learn by *doing* instead of just hearing about how something is done. Everyone listens closely to the instructor's lesson in reading the charts and compass, because they know that by the end of the course they will have to navigate and sail the boat themselves.

The students work together to chart a course to sail out of Rockland Harbor. Everyone has a job to do. One student points them in the right direction by sighting across a compass that is set inside a wooden box. After the anchor is lifted and the sails are raised, one student will keep a hand on the *tiller* and steer the boat. Others will tend the sails.

For several days, the watch sails in Penobscot Bay, navigating through narrow island passages and rowing the boat when the wind dies. At the captain's call "Come to oars! Prepare to give way!" four students unlash oars and set them in place. With the call "Give way!" the rowing begins.

During the night an *anchor watch* is kept. Every two hours a pair of students takes a shift, staying awake to check on the anchor lines to be sure the boat does not drift.

Finally, the watch arrives at Hurricane Island. For the next four days, their morning begins with a warm-up stretch and two-mile run around the island, followed by a dip into the cool Atlantic Ocean. At low tide this jump can be as much as 15 feet! At first, the dip is scary, but most students soon come to enjoy it, shouting war whoops as they leave the pier.

After breakfast everyone meets to listen to a
humorous or inspirational reading and to discuss
the day's activities. An instructor may read a
passage from Mark Twain on the unpredictable
New England weather. Members of a watch
scheduled to go on a rock climb may talk about
their fears. Sharing concerns ahead of time helps
all the students realize they are "in the same boat."

At an old granite quarry, students are taught basic *bouldering* techniques for rock climbing. Starting on low rocks, students learn to push their feet against the rock and use the friction between the rock and their feet to move. The process is similar to walking up a steep ramp. They also learn to *mantle up* onto rocks by pushing up on their arms and swinging a foot onto the ledge.

During a later rock-climbing session, students learn to protect each other by attaching ropes to their harnesses and *belaying* each other. As one person climbs, the other sits securely at the top of the cliff and takes the rope up, keeping tension on it. The climber doesn't climb the rope—he climbs the rock, with the safety rope as back-up.

On a larger rock face, students really put bouldering skills to work. Imagine standing on a narrow ledge, wide enough for only a few toes, and looking around for another ledge to grab with your fingers. Slowly you make your way up, one move at a time. Lunging for a good handhold or gripping the rock only tires you out. The secret is patience, good balance, and steady movement.

Once the climbers reach the top, they must *rappel* down to the ground. Still tied to ropes, they slowly lower themselves backward down the cliff. This is a scary process, but once it is mastered, climbers may even stop to admire the view. Far below the 80-foot quarry wall lies the pond, and just a few yards beyond that, Penobscot Bay.

Just when the students think they can relax, the instructors take them to the ropes course, an aerial Jungle gym of logs, ropes, and wires, where balance is the key to success. After putting their helmets on and tying themselves into harnesses, students start to climb up into the trees.

All members of the watch get to climb ladders,
walk on logs, and work their way like spiders
across a maze of ropes, some suspended as high as
35 feet in the air. Breathing slowly and taking one
step at a time, each student makes progress.

Before students leave on another sailing expedition, they purposely capsize a pulling boat in the anchorage at Hurricane Island. This exercise helps them learn to handle stressful situations by working together as a team. The students and instructor take an empty boat 100 yards away from the pier, stand together on the edge of the boat, and slowly pull the boat over until it is upside down.

After they pull the boat right side up again, they must bail the water out. The process may seem endless, but with everyone working, it is really only five minutes from capsize to recovery! With teamwork, the boat is soon dry again, and students swim back to the pier.

When students have learned how to handle the pulling boat under all conditions, they get to plan a four- to five-day expedition by themselves. They decide where they want to go and how long it will take them to get there. Instructors then give advanced lessons in navigation and offer "local knowledge" they have about the areas they will visit.

Instructors let the students run the boat as much as possible on the expedition. The students have made up their *itineraries*, or daily schedules, and have decided where they will anchor and who will be captain and navigator each day. Now it is time to load the boat with supplies, which range from food to first-aid equipment. Some students practice first-aid techniques while they wait for the command to cast off.

Every Outward Bound course teaches students about the natural world. Here, an instructor and student closely examine a tidal pool—a micro-environment of starfish, mussels, rock crabs, and many kinds of seaweed. Instructors teach students what plants and animals are edible, so the members of a watch can make a whole meal right out of a tidal pool.

The fruit of the *rosa rugosa* is called *rose hips*. It is used to make tea and jelly. *Sea urchins* are tough, spiny, globe-shaped animals. The *roe*, or eggs, of the sea urchin are considered a tasty delicacy in many parts of the world.

In addition to learning to appreciate the natural environment, Outward Bound students also learn to care about other people. As part of this approach, they may offer a day of service to the community. This watch is visiting a small island town to help paint a 100-year-old schoolhouse. Members of other watches may pick up trash from a populated shoreline or take an overnight shift at the radio rescue station on Hurricane Island.

While students are on sailing expeditions, they cook their own meals. When they are on Hurricane Island, however, they join other watches in the mess hall for specialties prepared by the galley crew. Typical dinners are fresh fish, pizza, and stir-fried vegetables with seaweed. The watches take turns cleaning up, sometimes for as many as 100 people!

The next day, students face *initiatives*, or exercises in which they must solve a common problem. One initiative, "The Wall," calls for students to scale a 12-foot wooden wall with no footholds or handholds. Every group has a new strategy for getting over the top. Some stand on each other's shoulders, while others jump up to catch outstretched hands. Still others reach down to help.

Another initiative is the "Spider's Web," in which every member of the watch must pass through a tangle of ropes *without touching any of the ropes.* This involves steady hands and especially careful planning, because every hole that someone passes through is "closed off" to other students. The last person passing through has a rough time.

After days of living closely together as a group, most students are ready for some solo days on an island. Each student is given a *tarp*, or ground cover, and training in how to *forage* for food. Students are also checked daily by instructors, who patrol the area in a motor boat. Once a makeshift shelter has been built, most students spend their solo time exploring the island, thinking about how the course is going, and figuring out how to keep warm.

When solo is over, students are glad to see each other again and join in a group hug. Much to everyone's surprise, discussion usually centers on what people were thinking about during their time alone, rather than the practical concerns of pitching a rainproof tarp and staying warm.

Just before the course is over, students do stretching exercises and then run a 6-mile *marathon* around the rocky perimeter of Hurricane Island. This final run inspires students to meet personal running goals. This may mean setting a time to beat, running at a steady pace, or helping a friend over hills.

After running the homestretch on rocky Barge Head, which looks out on Penobscot Bay, students cross the finish line and are greeted by other members of the watch. No matter who finished first or last, everyone in the watch has completed the course, and that is a true accomplishment.

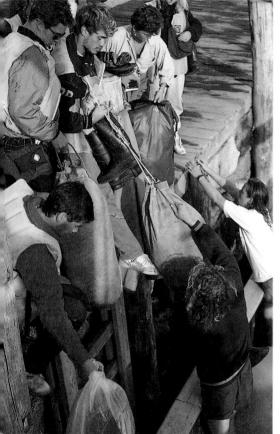

At last, it is time for students to leave Hurricane Island. For each member of the watch, saying goodbye is different. For some, it is a time for laughter and sharing memories. For others, it is a time to find a quiet place to rest and reflect about the meaning of these past 18 days. But no matter how they say goodbye, Outward Bound students know they are ready for whatever new adventures lie ahead.